Catastrophic Storms

W9-AXW-810

by Michael Sandler

TABLE OF CONTENTS

Words To Think About

Characteristics

destroys homes

harms people

?

catastrophic storm

What do you think the words **catastrophic storm** mean?

Examples

hurricane

tornado

?

atmosphere

What do you think the word **atmosphere** means?

Latin: atmos (vapor or gas)

Latin: sphaera (sphere or ball)

meteorologist

What do you think the word **meteorologist** means?

Who is a **meteorologist**?

scientist — ? — weather reporter

What does a **meteorologist** do?

studies storms — ? — predicts weather

iv

Introduction

Storms happen all the time. Storms can ruin a picnic. They can wash out a baseball game. Usually storms bring wind, rain, or snow. Most storms do little damage. **Catastrophic** (kat-uh-STRAWF-ic) storms are different. Catastrophic storms can do a lot of damage. They can shut down roads, trains, and airports. They can destroy homes. They can lift boats out of the ocean. Worst of all, these storms can kill people.

Catastrophic storms come in three types. The first type is a **hurricane** (HUHR-ih-kayn). A hurricane is a mix of heavy wind and rain. Hurricanes begin at sea. If they hit land, they can do a lot of harm.

The second type of catastrophic storm is a **tornado** (tohr-NAY-doh). Tornadoes are smaller than hurricanes but more powerful. Tornadoes make the strongest winds on Earth. They destroy everything in their paths.

The third kind of storm is a **blizzard** (BLIH-zuhrd). Blizzards are a blinding mix of wind, cold, and snow. They can bury whole towns in snow.

Scientists who study weather are called **meteorologists** (MEE-tee-uh-RAHL-uh-jists). Every day, meteorologists learn more about what causes these storms. Read on to find out more about catastrophic storms. Learn how nature makes them.

▲ snowstorm in Bodie, California

Hurricanes

What Is a Hurricane?

A hurricane is a huge storm. Hurricanes have heavy rain and strong winds. They are much bigger than regular thunderstorms. A regular storm has winds of 20 miles (32 kilometers) per hour. A hurricane can have winds of 150 miles (241 kilometers) per hour or more.

A regular storm may cover 2 square miles (5.2 square kilometers). A hurricane can cover hundreds or thousands of square miles. A regular storm may last an hour. A hurricane may last for a week or longer.

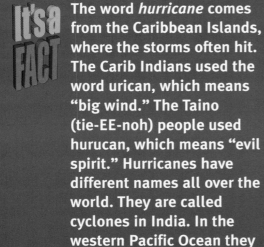

It's a FACT

The word *hurricane* comes from the Caribbean Islands, where the storms often hit. The Carib Indians used the word urican, which means "big wind." The Taino (tie-EE-noh) people used hurucan, which means "evil spirit." Hurricanes have different names all over the world. They are called cyclones in India. In the western Pacific Ocean they are called typhoons. In Australia they are called willie willies.

▲ A person struggles to walk in Hurricane Andrew.

Hurricanes do not just happen anywhere. They begin over warm ocean water near the equator. They can travel for hundreds of miles. Sometimes they hit land. When hurricanes hit land they can be catastrophic.

Hurricanes come at certain times of year. North of the equator, hurricane season lasts from June through November. South of the equator, the hurricane season lasts from November through April.

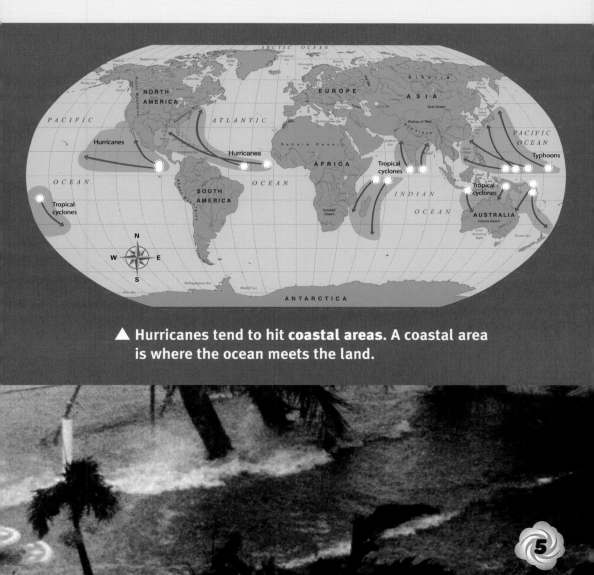

▲ Hurricanes tend to hit **coastal areas**. A coastal area is where the ocean meets the land.

How a Hurricane Is Born

1 High-Pressure Area	**2** Low-Pressure Area	**3** Storm Clouds	**4** Spiral	**5** Strong Winds
Air warms up and collects moisture as it moves down toward the surface of the ocean.	Warm, moist air from a high-pressure area moves into the low-pressure area. The air rises and cools. More air moves in to take the rising air's place.	Water droplets in the rising air collect and form storm clouds.	Because of the rotation of Earth, storm clouds spin up in a spiral.	Air flows into the storm clouds from the bottom and from the top. This flowing air creates strong winds.

1

2

3

4–5

When the winds near the center of a storm blow between 23–39 miles (27–62.8 kilometers) per hour, it is called a tropical depression. If the winds grow to between 39–73 miles (62.8–117.5 kilometers) per hour, it is called a tropical storm. If the winds reach 74 miles (119 kilometers) per hour, a hurricane is born.

How Hurricanes Form

Hurricanes need two special conditions to form. The first is warm ocean water of at least 80° Fahrenheit (27° Celsius). That is why hurricanes have seasons. Ocean waters only get warm enough at certain times of the year. The second condition is low air pressure.

Air near Earth's surface is always under pressure. The pressure comes from the **atmosphere** (AT-muhs-feer). The atmosphere is the layers of gas that surround Earth. When the atmosphere's weight presses down hard on the surface air, there is high pressure. Sometimes the atmosphere presses down with less force. Surface air can rise more easily. When this happens, there is low air pressure.

1. Solve This

A tropical depression has winds of 25 miles (40.2 kilometers) per hour. The storm grows stronger. A day later, winds are blowing 40 miles (64 kilometers) per hour faster. What is the storm now? Is it a tropical depression, a tropical storm, or a hurricane?

Math ✔ Point

What steps did you follow to answer the question?

Now you know how a hurricane is born. Look at the diagram below. You can see the hurricane's different parts.

Inside a Hurricane

Spiral Bands	Eyewall	Eye
The spiral bands are areas of clouds, wind, and rain that extend further out from the center of a hurricane.	Surrounding the eye is the eyewall, the storm's strongest part. It is a wall of swirling clouds. Here, the hurricane's fiercest winds blow and the heaviest rain falls.	At a hurricane's center is the eye. It is a cloudless area where the winds are somewhat calm.

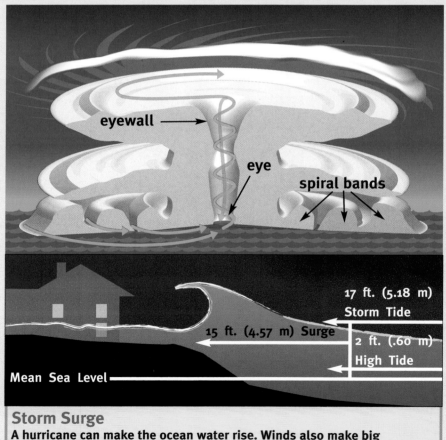

eyewall

eye

spiral bands

17 ft. (5.18 m)
Storm Tide

15 ft. (4.57 m) Surge

2 ft. (.60 m)
High Tide

Mean Sea Level

Storm Surge
A hurricane can make the ocean water rise. Winds also make big waves. When a high wall of ocean water hits shore, it is called a **storm surge (STORM SERJ)**.

Catastrophic Hurricanes

Meteorologists use a scale to measure how strong a hurricane is. The scale has five levels. The levels, or categories, are based on wind speed. The categories are also based on how high the ocean water rises.

A hurricane of category 3 or higher can be catastrophic. The wind can hurl trees through the air. It can tear roofs off houses. It can destroy mobile homes. The storm surge can smash things on the coast. The heavy rain can cause floods and mudslides.

It's a FACT

Storm surges account for about ninety percent of all hurricane-related deaths.

Category	Wind Speed	Surge Height
1	74–95 mph (119–153 kph)	4–5 feet (1.22–1.82 meters)
2	96–110 mph (154–177 kph)	6–8 feet (1.83–2.73 meters)
3	111–130 mph (178–209 kph)	9–12 feet (2.74–3.95 meters)
4	131–155 mph (210–250 kph)	13–18 feet (3.96–5.49 meters)
5	156+ mph (251+ kph)	18+ feet (5.49+ meters)

Hurricane Katrina, 2005

Hurricane Katrina was the biggest storm to ever hit the United States. Katrina killed more than 1,000 people. It caused billions of dollars of damage. Most of the damage was in Louisiana, Mississippi, and Florida. Here is the story of the storm.

▼ New Orleans before Hurricane Katrina

▲ New Orleans after Hurricane Katrina

August 24: Meteorologists start to track tropical storm Katrina. They send out a hurricane warning to people in Florida.

August 25: Katrina becomes a category 1 storm. The storm hits Florida. It has winds of 80 miles (128.8 kilometers) per hour. Eleven people are killed.

August 27: Katrina is now a category 3 storm. Its winds are 115 mph (185 kph). The mayor of New Orleans tells everyone to leave the city. The waters of a nearby lake may break through the levees (LEV-eez). Levees are huge walls built along a lake or river to protect land from flooding. People rush to leave the city. Highways are jammed.

August 28: Katrina is now a category 5 storm. Shelters are set up for people in New Orleans. Thousands go to the Superdome football stadium.

August 29: Katrina hits the Louisiana coast just after 7:00 A.M. The winds rip holes in the roof of the Superdome.

August 30: Two of the levees on the lake break. Water pours out. In hours, more than eighty percent of New Orleans is under water. In some places the water is more than twenty feet high. People sit on rooftops to get away from the rising water.

After Katrina

August 31: In the Gulf of Mexico, five oil rigs are missing. Two more have broken free from their anchors.

September 1: More than 80,000 people are in shelters. Many others have no water, food, or electricity.

September 2: Many people are hurt or dying. President Bush tours the area. He promises to get more help.

▲ homes in Louisiana destroyed by Hurricane Katrina

It's a FACT

To track hurricanes, meteorologists give each tropical storm a name. The first storm of the season gets a name beginning with the letter A. The second gets a name that begins with the letter B. The process continues through the alphabet. For many years, hurricanes were only given women's names. Since 1979, men's names have also been used.

What's Next?

Two years later, much still needs to be done. Many people have not been able to go home. Some people will never return. Years may pass before some areas are rebuilt. Some places will never be the same.

2. Solve This

Use the table below to answer the following question.

Is the following statement true or false? Before Katrina, Hurricane Andrew caused more damage than hurricanes Hugo, Agnes, Betsy, and Camille combined.

HURRICANE	YEAR	CATEGORY	DAMAGE*
Andrew	1992	5	$34,955,000,000
Hugo	1989	4	$ 9,740,000,000
Agnes	1972	1	$ 8,621,000,000
Betsy	1965	3	$ 8,517,000,000
Camille	1969	5	$ 6,992,000,000

*rounded to the nearest million dollars

Tornadoes

What Is a Tornado?

A tornado is a very strong windstorm. It is much smaller than a hurricane. It is usually less than a mile (1.6 kilometers) in width. A tornado looks like a long, thin tube or a funnel. It may be wider at the top than at the bottom. It is actually a spinning column of air.

A tornado is often called a twister. That is because of its twisting, spinning motion. The twisting air sucks up dirt and dust. The dirt makes a tornado look gray or even black. A tornado is also very noisy. People say a tornado sounds like a train roaring down the tracks.

▲ Seventy-five percent of the world's tornadoes occur in the United States.

Tornadoes can last from a few minutes to an hour. Most tornadoes travel only a short distance. Few travel farther than 100 miles (about 161 kilometers).

The winds of a tornado can be stronger than the winds of a hurricane. Tornado winds have been measured at 300 to 350 miles (482 to 563 kilometers) per hour. Meteorologists can predict, or tell ahead of time, where a hurricane will go. Tornadoes are harder to predict. A tornado may move at 60 miles (96.5 kilometers) per hour or stay spinning in one spot.

Tornadoes can happen anywhere. Most take place inland during the spring and summer. In the United States, tornadoes occur in every state. Most happen in the Midwest between the Rocky Mountains and Appalachian Mountains.

It's a FACT

A waterspout is a tornado that forms or passes over the water.

How Tornadoes Form

Like a hurricane, a tornado needs warm, wet air to form. In the United States, warm air often blows up from the Gulf of Mexico. This warm air meets cooler, drier air from the north. Thunderstorms form where the warm and cool air meet. Tornadoes grow out of the thunderstorms.

How a Tornado Is Born

1 Cool Air

Cool air forces warm air up, creating an updraft.

2 Warm Air

Moisture from the warm air forms thunderclouds. Water droplets in the clouds become rain.

3

There are now downward winds from the heavy rain.

4

Near the ground, winds racing into and away from the storm create a spinning column of air.

5

The updraft from the thunderstorm tilts this column up toward the sky. It becomes vertical, extending from the ground into the storm.

6

More air rushes into the column. The rotating winds get stronger. Water vapor from the falling rain creates a spinning funnel-shaped cloud. The tornado is born.

Cool Air Mass

Warm Air Mass

Catastrophic Tornadoes

Scientists use the Fujita (foo-GEE-tuh) Wind Damage Scale to measure tornadoes. The scale measures tornadoes from F0 to F5. F0 and F1 tornadoes are weak. F2 and F3 tornadoes are strong. F4 and F5 tornadoes can be catastrophic.

The strongest tornadoes can lift a car. They can suck the roof off of a house. People can be sucked up by tornadoes, but most injuries are caused by flying objects.

▲ scientist Ted Fujita

The Fujita Scale

Category	Wind Speed	Damage
F0	72 mph (116 kph)	**Light:** branches broken, chimneys damaged
F1	73–112 mph (117–180 kph)	**Moderate:** cars pushed off roads, mobile homes overturned
F2	113–157 mph (181–253 kph)	**Considerable:** mobile homes smashed, small objects become missiles
F3	158–206 mph (254–332 kph)	**Severe:** roofs and walls torn from well-built houses, trees uprooted, medium-size objects become missiles
F4	207–260 mph (333–418 kph)	**Devastating:** houses destroyed, large objects become missiles
F5	261–319 mph (419–513 kph)	**Incredible:** strong houses thrown through the air, cars hurled 100 yards (about 91 meters)

The Tri-State Tornado

On March 18, 1925, a bad thunderstorm developed in Missouri. Out of the storm burst an F5 tornado. The tornado headed northeast. It kept going for three and a half hours. That tornado set a record.

▲ The Tri-State storm destroyed everything in its path.

The tornado passed through three states. The storm traveled 219 miles (342 kilometers). It passed through Missouri, Illinois, and Indiana. People called it the "Tri-State Tornado."

The twister had winds of 300 miles (482.7 kilometers) per hour. Trees and homes were hurled through the air. The Tri-State Tornado killed nearly 700 people. It was the deadliest twister in American history.

3. Solve This

Use the bar graph at right to answer the questions.

a. What percentage of tornadoes are F4s and F5s?
b. What percentage of tornado-related deaths are caused by F4s and F5s?
c. Which categories of tornadoes cause about 30% of tornado-related deaths?

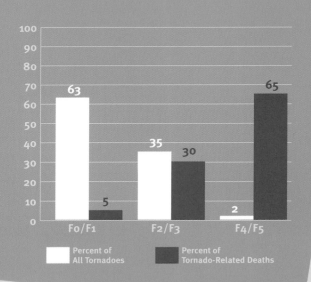

▲ This building in Ohio was ripped in half by a tornado.

The Super Outbreak

The only thing scarier than one tornado is a group of them. A single thunderstorm can produce a "family" of tornadoes. Certain weather can produce tornado outbreaks across many states.

One such outbreak took place on April 3, 1974. Within one day, thirteen states reported tornadoes. The final count was 148 tornadoes. More than 5,000 people were hurt. More than 300 people died. The storms caused about $600 million in damage.

The worst tornado blew into a small town in Ohio. This storm had winds of more than 260 miles (418 kilometers) per hour. Nearly half of the town's homes were damaged or destroyed.

More people might have died. During the Super Outbreak, weather reports saved lives. People watching the weather reports went to shelters and were safe.

The Wizard of Oz

What's the most famous tornado that never really happened? Probably the twister that sucked up Dorothy and her dog Toto. The tornado in the book and movie was fiction. But in real life, a person can be sucked up into a tornado.

19

Tornado Alley

One part of America gets more tornadoes than anywhere else in the world. This area is known as Tornado Alley.

Why does this area get so many twisters? Cold air from the Rocky Mountains flows over the flat plains in this region. The cold air meets warm, wet air from the Gulf of Mexico. Thunderstorms take place where the cold and warm air meet. These thunderstorms create tornadoes.

On May 3, 1999, more than forty twisters hit Oklahoma. The wind speed of one tornado was 318 miles (512 kilometers) per hour. These winds were the strongest winds ever recorded on Earth.

▼ The average tornado lasts for just seven minutes. It is most likely to strike in the late afternoon.

▼ The shaded area is Tornado Alley.

Tornado Safety

People were once told to open their windows if a tornado came near. The idea was to make the air pressure inside their car or house the same as the air pressure outside.

Today, experts say to forget about the windows.

A tornado will blast the windows to pieces. Instead, go to a safe place.

Where are the safest places? Get far away from any windows. Go down to the basement if you can. Try to cover yourself with thick padding. A mattress or a few blankets will work.

Point

Think About It

Which do you consider more frightening— a tornado or a hurricane? Why?

4. Solve This

The year 1992 was record-breaking for tornadoes. In the United States, 1,297 twisters were reported. Of those, 420 tornadoes struck four Tornado Alley states: Oklahoma, Texas, Nebraska, and Kansas. How many tornadoes struck in other states?

Math Point

What strategy did you use to solve the problem? Did you add, subtract, multiply, or divide?

Blizzards

What Is a Blizzard?

Most snowstorms are not blizzards. A true blizzard must pass three tests. First, it must have winds of at least 35 miles (56.3 kilometers) per hour. Second, the temperature must be below 20° Fahrenheit (-7° Celsius). Third, a person in the storm must only be able to see as far as a quarter mile (about .40 of a kilometer).

Blizzards can take place wherever it is cold. Huge blizzards can cover large sections of the country. Blizzards often happen at the beginning or end of winter.

Everyday Science

The wind of a blizzard blows heat away from a person's body. The effect is called **wind chill.** Low wind chill can cause **frostbite** and hypothermia (high-poh-THERM-ee-uh). Frostbite is a loss of feeling in the fingers, toes, or other parts of the body from the cold. During hypothermia, human body temperatures become dangerously low. Hypothermia can be deadly if it is not treated quickly.

5. Solve This

Use the table below to solve the problems.

a. The temperature is 20° Fahrenheit. The winds are 35 miles per hour. What is the wind chill?

b. The temperature drops another 10 degrees and the winds speed up to 50 miles per hour. What is the wind chill now?

TEMPERATURE (Fahrenheit)

WIND (mph)	30	25	20	15	10	5	0
5	25	19	13	7	1	-5	-11
10	21	15	9	3	-4	-10	-16
15	19	13	6	0	-7	-13	-19
20	17	11	4	-2	-9	-15	-22
25	16	9	3	-4	-11	-17	-24
30	15	8	1	-5	-12	-19	-26
35	14	7	0	-7	-14	-21	-27
40	13	6	-1	-8	-15	-22	-29
45	12	5	-2	-9	-16	-23	-30
50	12	4	-3	-10	-17	-24	-31
55	11	4	-3	-11	-18	-25	
60	10	3	-4	-11	-19	-26	

How Blizzards Form

Blizzards are fairly rare. Winter air is cold and dry. Cold, dry air does not make much snow. A blizzard needs a mixture of warm and very cold air to form. That is why blizzards form at the beginning or end of winter. The air can be slightly warmer at that time.

How a Blizzard Is Born

① Warm Air	② Warm Front	③ Cool Air
A mass of warm air, coming from tropical areas, runs into a mass of cold air from a polar region.	The leading edge of the warm air mass is called a warm front. The warm front air is lighter than the colder air that it hits. So the warm air rises up above the cold air.	Water vapor in the warm air condenses into colder air in the clouds. Then it falls as snow.

cool air

warm front

warm air

Catastrophic Blizzards

A bad blizzard has winds of 45 miles (72 kilometers) per hour or greater. Temperatures can be 10° Fahrenheit (12° Celsius) or below.

In bad blizzards people can see almost nothing. This is called a **whiteout**. The ground is white, the sky is white, and the air is white. It is easy to get lost during a whiteout. Flashlights or headlights do not work. Light just reflects off the snow.

▼ During this 1997 blizzard, Indiana motorists had to leave their vehicles on the highway.

Bad blizzards can drop 20 inches (50.8 centimeters) of snow or more. The wind can blow the snow into giant drifts. The snow is so heavy that roofs collapse and power lines snap.

INTERSTATE
40

No one can drive during a blizzard. Planes cannot take off or land. People are often stranded and may lose heat in their homes just when they need it most.

The Schoolchildren's Blizzard

On January 12, 1888, a mild winter's day in the Great Plains took a turn for the worse. Temperatures dropped 20 degrees in just a few minutes. The winds grew stronger. Heavy snow began to fall.

Many children were at school. Some children tried to make it home. These children got lost in the whiteout. It was very cold. Some children froze to death. In all, 235 people died. This blizzard became known as the "Schoolchildren's Blizzard."

▲ More than 200 people died in the "Schoolchildren's Blizzard."

The Blizzard of 1888

Another blizzard that year was even worse. On March 11, a snowstorm began to pound the East Coast and the Atlantic Ocean. The storm lasted for nearly three days. More than 4 feet (1.2 meters) of snow fell in some places.

Cities like New York, Boston, and Philadelphia shut down. Fierce winds built up tall snowdrifts. Some snowdrifts reached 50 feet (about 15 meters) high. The streets and railways were buried in snow. People were trapped in their homes. Some people were trapped on ships.

▲ The Great Blizzard of 1996 covered much of the East Coast in record amounts of snow.

More than 400 people died in the Blizzard of 1888. Many who died were on ships. Two hundred ships sank during the storm.

The Great Blizzard of 1996

In January 1996, a huge blizzard hit the East Coast. States from Virginia to Maine were covered in snow. Schools and offices were closed. Why was the snow so heavy? The blizzard stayed in one place for a long time. A cold air mass to the north kept it locked in.

Careers in Science

Meteorologists can have many different jobs. They might report weather conditions and make weather forecasts on TV. They might study how storms are formed. Some meteorologists work to develop better early warning systems about the storms.

Meteorologists might collect information about how weather is changing. They study global warming, the long-term heating up of Earth's atmosphere.

The Great Blizzard of 1996 affected more than fifty million people. Planes could not fly, so travelers slept in airports. Roads were closed to most traffic. At least 154 people died because of the storm.

▲ A New Yorker clears a path during the Great Blizzard of 1996.

RECORD SNOWFALLS

City	Great Blizzard of 1996 Snowfall	Previous Record Amount of Snowfall
Philadelphia, PA	30.7 in (77.9 cm)	21.3 in (54.1 cm)
Newark, NJ	27.8 in (70.6 cm)	22.6 in (57.4 cm)
Washington, D.C.	24.6 in (62.5 cm)	22.8 in (57.9 cm)
New York City	20.2 in (51.3 cm)	26.4 in (67.1 cm)

Conclusion

Catastrophic storms do great harm. These storms can take many lives. Hurricanes combine the power of the wind and the sea. Tornadoes destroy with the planet's most violent winds. Blizzards are a deadly mix of wind, snow, and cold.

Many terrible storms have struck the United States in the past. Many more will strike in the future. Meteorologists cannot stop the storms from coming. They can warn people before a storm arrives. Today, fewer people lose their lives to storms than in the past.

Answers to Solve This

1. page 7:
A tropical storm.
Math checkpoint: To get this answer, add 40 to 25. Then compare the result (65) to the wind speed for each type of storm.

2. page 13:
a. True. Add the figures for hurricanes Hugo, Agnes, Betsy, and Camille ($33,870,000,000). Then compare the result with the damage amount for Hurricane Andrew ($34,955,000,000).

3. page 18:
a. 2%. Find the bar symbol for percentage of all tornadoes. Then look at the bar marked F4/F5.

b. 65%. Find the bar symbol for percentage of all tornado-related deaths. Then look at the bar marked F4/F5.

c. F2/F3. Find 30% in the bar graph. Determine which category of tornado it corresponds with.

4. page 21: 877.
Math checkpoint: To get this answer, subtract 420 from 1297.

5. page 23:
a. 0 degrees F.
b. −17 degrees F.

Glossary

atmosphere (AT-muhs-feer) the mixture of gases that surrounds Earth (page 7)

blizzard (BLIH-zuhrd) a heavy snowstorm with very strong winds (page 3)

catastrophic (kat-uh-STRAWF-ic) capable of causing great damage and loss of life (page 2)

coastal area (KOHST-uhl AYR-ee-uh) land that is near the ocean (page 5)

frostbite (frawst-BYTE) injury to body parts, such as fingers and toes, that are exposed to the cold (page 22)

hurricane (HUHR-ih-kayn) a storm with very strong winds and heavy rain (page 2)

meteorologist (MEE-tee-uh-RAHL-uh-jist) a scientist who studies weather and climate patterns (page 3)

storm surge (STORM SERJ) a wall of ocean water pushed toward shore by a hurricane (page 8)

tornado (tohr-NAY-doh) a powerful storm with winds that whirl in a dark cloud shaped like a funnel (page 3)

whiteout (WYTE-owt) a complete loss of visibility that can occur during a blizzard (page 25)

wind chill (WIHND CHIHLL) the combined cooling effect of cold air and wind (page 22)

Index